# KNOWLEDGE ENCYCLOPEDIA
# MIDDLE AGES
# WORLD HISTORY

© Wonder House Books 2022

All rights reserved. No part of this book may be reproduced or transmitted in any form by any means, electronic or mechanical, including photocopying and recording, or by any information storage and retrieval system except as may be expressly permitted in writing by the publisher.

(An imprint of Prakash Books)

contact@wonderhousebooks.com

**Disclaimer:** The information contained in this encyclopedia has been collated with inputs from subject experts. All information contained herein is true to the best of the Publisher's knowledge. Maps are only indicative in nature

ISBN : 9789354401312

# Table of Contents

| | |
|---|---:|
| The Middle Ages | 3 |
| The Barbarian Invasions | 4–5 |
| Feudal Europe | 6–7 |
| The Byzantine Empire | 8 |
| The Holy Roman Empire | 9 |
| The Rise of Catholicism | 10–11 |
| The Rise of Islam | 12–13 |
| The Golden Age of Islam | 14–15 |
| Saxons and Normans | 16–17 |
| The Hundred Years' War | 18 |
| Medieval Africa | 19 |
| The Crusades | 20–21 |
| Boyars and Magyars | 22–23 |
| Mongol Hordes | 24–25 |
| The Kingdoms of China | 26–27 |
| Medieval India | 28–29 |
| Samurai and Shogun | 30–31 |
| Word Check | 32 |

# THE MIDDLE AGES

**The fall of the Roman Empire marks the beginning of the European Middle Ages.** This period lasted roughly from the 5th century to the 15th. The empire in Western Europe split into a number of kingdoms that would eventually give rise to our modern nations. This was, however, a time of poverty, disease, and religious wars like the Crusades. Eastern Europe flourished under the Byzantine and later Islamic empires. Further to the east, Asia had its own progressive civilisations. However, people enjoyed religious freedom only under some rulers. Vigorous international trade flourished alongside art, science, and exploration in Asia. In this sense, the gloomy Middle Ages is a uniquely Western way of viewing the world.

▲ An illustration from the medieval French epic Song of Roland, written as a chanson de geste (song of heroic deeds), one of the oldest forms of French literature

# The Barbarian Invasions

**Between the 4th and 8th centuries, Europe witnessed the Migration Period.** German tribes moved west and east across Europe in search of new and fertile lands. They called it Völkerwanderung, meaning 'wandering of the peoples'. This led to many wars with the Roman Empire, which occupied these lands. Ultimately, the Germanic invasions led to the fall of the Empire and the onset of the Middle Ages.

##  The First Phase (300–500 CE)

In 367 CE, tribes called Picts, Scots, Saxons, and Franks attacked the Roman Empire. In 376 CE, the Visigoths—fleeing another aggressive Germanic tribe called the Huns—burst on to eastern Roman lands. Displeased, the Romans launched several battles against them. The Goths finally crushed the Roman army at Adrianople in 378 CE. As uneasy alliance was formed. The Germans (Goths) were given a place to live as long as they protected the borders from further invasions. The truce did not last long. The Goths rebelled and invaded Italy, **sacking** Rome in 410 CE and settling down in the **Iberian peninsula**. Over 406-07, other tribes fleeing the Huns invaded **Gaul** and reached as far as Spain. They included Vandals, Alani, Suebi and Burgundians. The Vandals later crossed Africa and set up, in Carthage, the first independent German state on Roman soil.

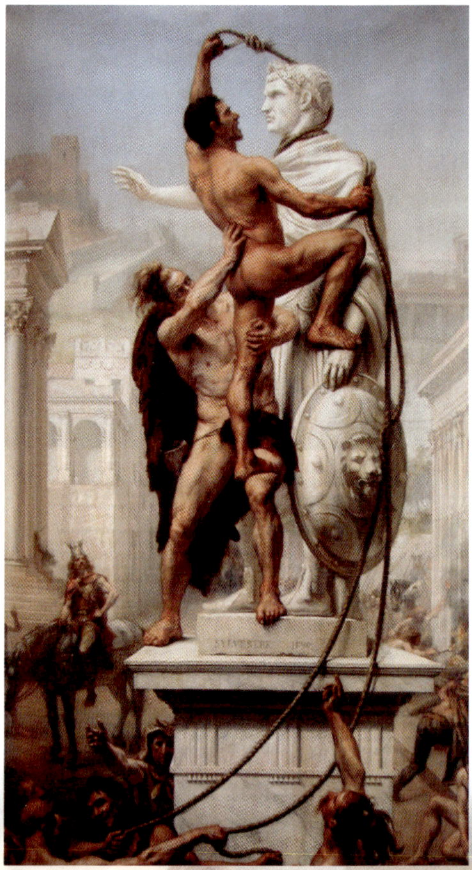

▶ In 410 CE, under the leadership of Alaric, the Visigoths sacked Rome. By this time, the Italian city of Ravenna had replaced Rome as the capital of the Western Roman Empire

▼ In 455 CE, Rome was sacked again, this time by Vandals; shown in art by 19th-century Russian painter Karl Briullov

# WORLD HISTORY — MIDDLE AGES

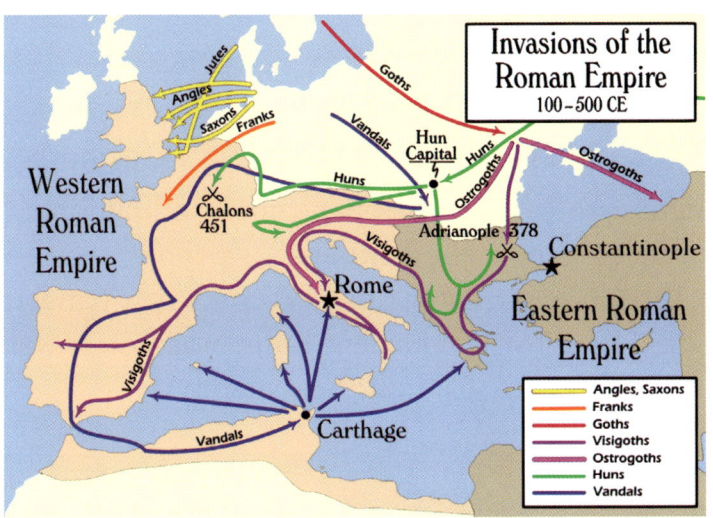

▲ A map of major invasions of the Roman Empire (100–500 CE), by the Angles, Saxons, Jutes, Franks, Goths, Visigoths, Ostrogoths, Huns, and Vandals

## The Second Phase (500–700 CE)

Tribes of people called Slavs settled Central and Eastern Europe during this period. The Bulgars, a now-Slavic group, had lived in Eastern Europe since the 2nd century. They conquered parts of the Byzantine Empire in the 7th century. The Lombards, another Germanic tribe, occupied northern Italy and gave it the name we still use today—Lombardy.

## ⊙ Incredible Individuals

A feared military general, Attila (406–53 CE) led the Hun Empire at its peak. He was a fierce threat to the Roman Empire, ruthlessly plundering great parts of Central and Western Europe, including Gaul and Italy. The only battle he ever lost was the Battle of the Catalaunian Plains in 451 CE. The story goes that Attila the Hun, the Scourge of God, died the night of his wedding to Ildiko, from excessive drinking! Others say he was killed by his wife Gudrun. His empire died soon after.

▲ The Feast of Attila shows a crowned Attila and his son Ellack being entertained by singers

## The Fall of Rome

In 476 CE, Ostrogoth general Odoacer (c. 433–93 CE) toppled Emperor Romulus Augustus and became King of Italy. Historians mark this date as the official fall of Rome. By this time, Vandals governed Africa, Visigoths ruled Spain, and Gaul was divided between various tribes, notably the Franks and Burgundians. However, the Eastern Roman Empire (Byzantium)—with its capital in Constantinople—continued until 1453!

▲ This gold bracteate (a medal worn as a jewel) belongs to the Migration Period. It is carved with what is possibly the Germanic God Odin

▶ Romulus Augustus gives up his crown to a victorious Odoacer

# Feudal Europe

**The unified government of the Roman Empire was gone.** Its land was divided up and ruled by Germanic lords and ladies, from manors and castles. **Serfs** and peasants farmed the land and served their lord. In return, the lord and his knights protected the people from invading forces. The lords owed allegiance to kings. This system of governing the land and its people is called feudalism. The kings vied for dominance with the Church. Merchants and craftsmen banded into professional groups called **guilds**. The scientific curiosity of ancient Rome was lost. It was replaced by blind faith in religion, specifically, in **patriarchal**, Catholic Christianity.

▲ *The feudal castle of Bouillon looms over a small town by the River Semois. In 1082, Godfrey of Bouillon sold the eerie fortress to raise money for the Crusades. He eventually became the first ruler of the Kingdom of Jerusalem*

## 💡 Isn't It Amazing!

Medieval knights had to follow a code of chivalry, which made them noble! They were loyal to one's lord, courteous to ladies, and upheld the Christian faith. Enemy knights were well-treated and exchanged for ransom, not killed outright. While chivalry was a wonderful idea, few knights truly followed it. It was popularised by wandering troubadours (musicians), whose ballads of heroic knights were immensely popular.

◂ *Medieval ladies watch a match between knights*

##  Medieval Women

Under Catholicism and feudalism, European women had almost no rights. A noblewoman was expected to obey her husband, bear children, and run the manor. She was rarely allowed a proper education and had no control over her money. Despite this, the Middle Ages witnessed exemplary women, like Empress Matilda (1102–67), who fought for the throne of England, and her daughter-in-law Eleanor of Aquitaine (c. 1122–1204), who joined the Crusades. The military genius Matilda of Tuscany (1046–1115) protected her lands (and the Pope) from the Holy Roman Emperor. Hildegard of Bingen (1098–1179) was a German **polymath** and Aethelflaed (c. 870–18 CE) was the influential Queen of Mercia.

▶ *Matilda was a powerful female ruler of Tuscany*

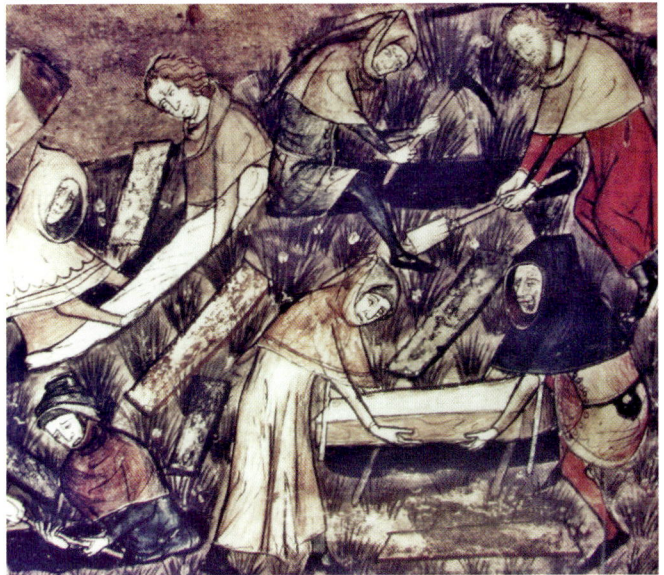

▲ *The people of Tournai bury victims of the Black Death, c. 1353*

##  The Black Death

Medieval medicine was a mix of folk remedies and faith. There was little science to it and doctors often caused more harm than good. An already poverty- and disease-ridden Europe was therefore decimated when the bubonic plague swept through it in the 14th century. It most likely came from Asia, travelling west on trading ships. Plague, aka the Black Death, caused red swellings that turned purple-black and oozy from thick, dark, smelly blood. So many died of it and so fast, that they couldn't all be buried, and corpses had to be piled up and burnt in pits. People thought it was a punishment from God. It was only in the 19th century that scientists realised plague was a bacterial infection and invented a vaccine against it.

##  The Little Ice Age

Around 1300, the planet began to cool, starting off a mini Ice Age that lasted till 1850. Changing climate led to bad harvests. People died from cold and famine. As populations fell, trade suffered leading to further poverty and many riots and rebellions.

##  The Peasants' Revolt of 1381

In England, young King Richard II was taken by surprise when—for the first time—farmers, labourers, and artisans rebelled against heavy taxes and low wages. Led by Wat Tyler, they marched to London, where they massacred Flemish merchants and destroyed a royal duke's palace. Forced to negotiate, the king promised them many things, including the abolition of serfdom. However, Tyler was later killed and the rebellion was mercilessly quashed.

▶ *An illustration from the Great Famine of 1315–1317 shows Death sitting on a manticore, whose long tail ends in the open, flaming maws of Famine*

# The Byzantine Empire (c. 330–1453 CE)

While the Roman Empire in the west was destroyed by Germanic tribes, it continued in the east with its capital at Constantinople. This Eastern Roman Empire came to be known as the Byzantine Empire. A centre of learning and trade, Constantinople was the largest and wealthiest city of Europe during its time.

◀ *A mosaic at Hagia Sofia in Constantinople shows the Virgin Mary and Christ. To their right stands Emperor Justinian I, with a model of the church; to the left is Emperor Constantine I, the founder of Constantinople in 306 CE*

##  East-West Schism

Over the 5th–11th centuries, the Byzantine church grew apart, over religious and political issues, from the church in Rome. They finally split in the **Schism** of 1054, forming the Eastern Christian churches (led by the patriarch of Constantinople, Michael Cerularius) and the Western church (led by Pope Leo IX). Both popes excommunicated each other. It was only in 1965 that Pope Paul VI and Patriarch Athenagoras I met in Jerusalem and lifted the excommunications!

###  In Real Life

The official language of the Byzantine Empire was Latin until 700 CE, when Emperor Heraclius changed it to Greek.

##  Empress Theodora (c. 497–548)

Born the daughter of a circus bear-keeper, talented, strong-willed Theodora married Justinian in 523 CE. When he was crowned emperor in 527 CE, he made her joint ruler. Theodora's skill in governance soon became apparent. In 532 CE, she helped quell the **Nika riots** and saved the empire. She also convinced Justinian to create laws upholding women's rights. This included giving women the right to make choices about their own bodies; the right to property in marriage, divorce, and widowhood; the right to justice against crime and violence, and a voice for the poor and downtrodden women.

▼ *Empress Theodora and her attendants are represented in beautiful mosaics completed a year before her death in 248 CE at the Church of San Vitale in Ravenna*

# The Holy Roman Empire

The Franks were western Germanic tribes that entered Roman lands gradually, in relative peace, over the 5th century. They were first united by King Clovis (r. 481/82–511 CE), who founded the Merovingian Dynasty and established its capital in Paris. The Merovingians officially ruled till 751, but by the 720s, they were only figureheads and the true power had been snatched away by a new family—the Carolingian Dynasty. The most famous Carolingian king is undoubtedly Charlemagne (c. 747–814). He was crowned the first emperor of what eventually became the Holy Roman Empire of the Middle Ages.

◄ *Crown of the Holy Roman Emperor created from gold, **cloisonné** enamel, precious stones, and pearls during the 10th century*

## Carolingian Heirs

King Charles I is better known as Charlemagne, meaning Charles the Great. He became king of the Franks in 768 CE and king of the Lombards in 774 CE. In 800, he became the first emperor of what would later be called the Holy Roman Empire. Charlemagne was the son of Pepin the Short, who began the official rule of the Carolingian Dynasty. After Charlemagne, his empire was divided, between three heirs, into the lands of West Francia, Lotharingia, and East Francia. The Holy Roman Empire began when Otto I of East Francia became emperor in 962.

## A Servant of the Crown

Pope Leo III wanted the church, and not the king, to be the top power in the land. He, therefore, hatched a plan to bring Charlemagne under the church's authority. On Christmas day, in 800 CE, he asked the king to kneel with him in prayer. As hundreds of people watched, Charlemagne knelt. Pope Leo silently placed a crown on his head and proclaimed him the first Holy Roman Emperor! The people cheered, considering this to be a great honour. But Charlemagne knew better. The title gave him no power or land, but made him a servant of the church. He never used the title and preferred to be called Emperor of the Franks and Lombards.

◄ *Coronation of Charlemagne as Holy Roman Emperor*

► *Stained-glass window portraying Otto I, the first ruler of the Holy Roman Empire, which lasted until Napoleon Bonaparte brought it to an end in 1806*

# The Rise of Catholicism

**With support from monarchs like Constantine I and Charlemagne, the Catholic Church soon gained enormous power.** At its centre was the Pope, who oversaw an army of cardinals, bishops, monks, and priests. They told the kings, nobles, and commoners what God wanted. People in the Middle Ages feared God so much, that they often did just as they were told to, by their religious leaders.

▲ Monasteries like the Abbey of Monte Casino, originally built by St. Benedict, were self-sufficient places where monks worked on fields, took care of cattle, and even made wine and cheese

▲ The son of a Roman senator, Pope Gregory I (c. 540–604) was a great early administrator of the Catholic Church and famously sent missions to convert England to Christianity

##  Monasticism

A monk is someone who lives his life in austerity and prayer. In 520 CE, Benedict of Nursia (c. 480–547 CE) stated that a priest could not marry, could not own goods, and had to obey his **abbot**. St. Benedict is considered the father of Western monasticism. Women who followed such rules became nuns. They lived in convents overseen by an **abbess**. Monks wore coarse brown robes and shaved their heads. Nuns wore a gown, a veil, and a white cloth—called a wimple—around their neck and face.

##  The Wealthy Church

Life was hard during the Middle Ages. People came to believe that if you followed certain rules, you would be safe and could even go to heaven. One of these rules involved donating land, jewellery, and money to the church, to make up for your sins. This was called 'buying an indulgence'. Such penance made the church rich. In fact, the church became so wealthy, that many nobles saw it as a good profession. Soon, it became common for leaders of the church to be aristocrats, who often put the interests of their powerful families before the interests of God and the common people. As the church became increasingly corrupt, the indulgence was used for nefarious purposes. The church even pardoned sins committed in its service, assuring God-fearing extremists that they would have a place in heaven!

◀ A manuscript from the 1490s condemns the church's distribution of indulgences (a way to reduce the punishment for your sin by paying the church) by associating it with Satan

##  The Inquisition

The Catholic church believed it was responsible for interpreting the word of God. Anyone else who tried to do so was considered as being tempted by the devil and was branded a heretic! To ensure that people obeyed the church, it set up the Inquisition. Priests of the Inquisition found and destroyed anyone who spoke against the church. The heretics were often mercilessly tortured and even burnt at the stake. It was one of the cruellest tools of subjugation in medieval times.

### Incredible Individuals

The brilliant poet-philosopher Dante Alighieri (1265–1321) was a rare light in the literary gloom of the European Middle Ages. His epic *Divine Comedy* was written in Italian at a time when Latin was considered the language of the educated. The poem is a journey through the Christian afterlife. It moves through three parts—Inferno (Hell), Purgatorio (**Purgatory**), and Paradiso (Heaven).

◀ *Dante Alighieri ruminates over a copy of his masterwork, the Divine Comedy*

▲ *The Inquisition prepares to burn heretics at the stake, c. 1493–1499*

##  St. Francis of Assisi

Friars were monks who travelled under vows of poverty, begging for food and shelter. The most famous was St. Francis of Assisi (1182–1226), who joined the Crusades with the hope to conquer the Muslim people with love rather than war. He was famous for his love of animals. Among his miracles is a story of him saving a village by taming a wolf. In 1220, Francis set up the first known **Nativity** scene to celebrate Christmas.

## The Western Schism

Over 1378–1417, the Catholic Church had two, sometimes three, popes at the same time! The French kings, who wished to influence the Church, had French popes who held court in Avignon. This schism ended in 1417 at the Council of Constance. The popes John XXIII and Gregory XII resigned. A third pope, Benedict XIII, was excommunicated. And a fresh, single pope, Martin V, was finally elected for all Catholics everywhere.

▶ *The final resting place of St. Francis of Assisi, the Basilica of San Francesco d'Assisi in Italy*

◀ *This Quran at the University of Birmingham is one of the oldest in the world, and dates to 568–645 CE*

# The Rise of Islam

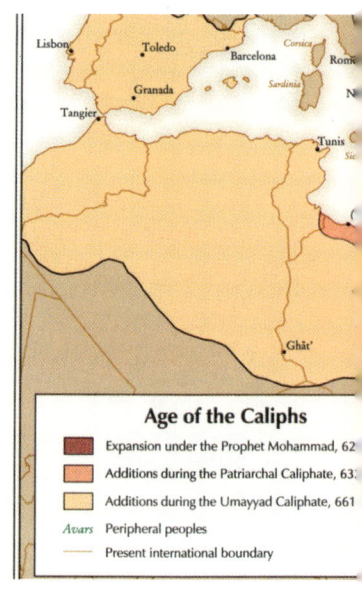

▲ *Expansion of Islam under the early Caliphs*

**Islam is a word meaning 'submission to God's will'.** The followers of Islam are called Muslims. The religion was founded in Arabia in the early 7th century by Prophet Muhammad (570–632 CE). Followers of Islam believe in one God, Allah, and in his divine words as given in their holy book, the *Quran*. After the Prophet passed away, Islamic scholars gathered his actions and sayings into additional texts known as the Hadith.

## The Rashidun Caliphs (632–661 CE)

After the Prophet's death, Islam came to be ruled by **caliphs** who were elected, or who took over by force. The first four caliphs are called Rashidun, meaning 'rightly guided'. First, there was Abu Bakr (573–634 CE) who had been Muhammad's father-in-law. He had the Prophet's teachings written down in the *Quran*. He was succeeded by Caliph Umar (c. 586–644 CE), another father-in-law of Muhammad's. Under Umar, Muslims conquered the greater part of the Byzantine Empire. Administrative offices were set up and Islam became a true nation. Its Arab armies conquered Mesopotamia, Syria and moved towards Persia and Egypt. Umar also established the Muslim calendar. He was, however, assassinated in 644 CE and Uthman, Muhammad's son-in-law, took over. In 656 CE, Uthman too was killed. His passing led to the First Fitna (Islamic civil war). Muhammad's cousin and son-in-law, Ali (c. 600–661 CE), was selected as the next caliph. He oversaw a tumultuous time for Islam. Despite this, Arab Muslims conquered large regions in the Middle East, including modern-day Iran and Iraq. Islam also spread across great swathes of Europe, Africa, and Asia.

◀ *The amazing Dome of the Rock in Jerusalem was first completed in 691–692 CE at the order of Umayyad Caliph Abd al-Malik, during the Second Fitna. The dome collapsed in 1015 and was rebuilt in 1022–1023*

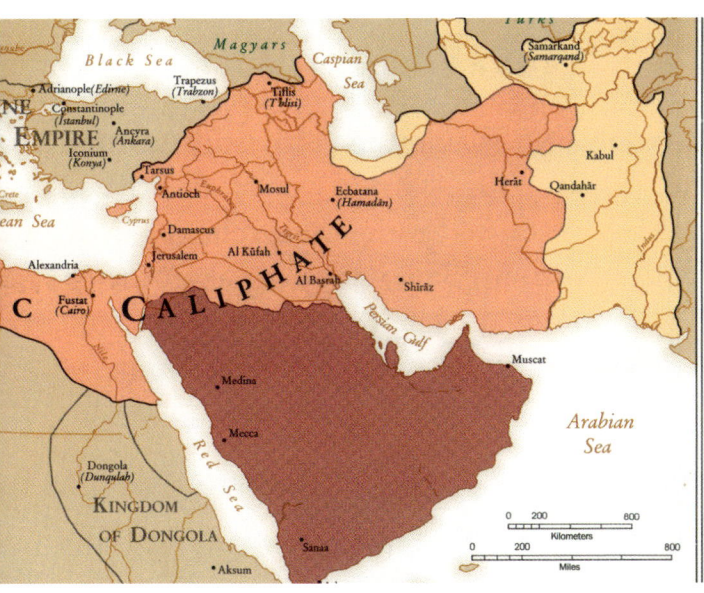

## 🐎 The Umayyad Caliphate (661–750 CE)

Ali and his supporters were eventually overthrown by Mu'awiya, governor of Syria and a relative of Uthman's. He established Damascus as the capital of the first Islamic dynasty, the Umayyad. With this, the caliph was no longer elected by his peers. The position was passed on within the family. The Umayyad Dynasty ruled from Damascus until 750; and later established another kingdom in Cordoba, Spain.

▲ *Siege* of Baghdad by Hulagu Khan shows the conquest and end of the Abbasid Caliphate at the hands of the Mongols

## 🐎 The Abbasid Caliphate (750–1258 CE)

The last Umayyad caliph was overthrown by a successful revolt that arose in Persia in 747 CE. It was led by descendants of al-Abbas, an uncle of the Prophet's. Unlike the Umayyads, who were interested in Africa and the West, the Abbasid caliphate—with its Persian sophistication and long history of empire building—looked eastwards. Baghdad, on the River Tigris, became the new capital. Over the next century, the empire grew into an international entity, powerful in commerce, industry, arts, and science. It was supported by strong caliphs such as al-Mans'ur (c. 709–75), Harun al-Rashid (c. 763–809), and al-Ma'mun (786–833). By the 10$^{th}$ century, Islam had spread across great swathes of land, stretching beyond Baghdad in the east, Cairo in the south-centre, and Cordoba in the west.

## ⭐ Incredible Individuals

The wonder and opulence of Harun al-Rashid's Baghdad is well known to us through the amazing book of Arabian fantasies, *A Thousand and One Nights*. Many details in these stories reflect the splendour of the Muslim court. This period was marked by peace and affability on the part of the caliphates. Harun al-Rashid had such international fame, Charlemagne's biographers record the mutual respect which was shared by the two emperors when they exchanged gifts.

▲ *Caliph Harun al-Rashid receives gifts at his court in Baghdad*

▲ *Arabic text of the fabulous A Thousand and One Nights*

# The Golden Age of Islam

While medieval Europe succumbed to superstition, poverty, and disease, the Islamic world flourished with attention given to trade, research, sciences, arts, and philosophy. The period between the 8th and 14th centuries is its golden age. It began with the reign of Harun al-Rashid and his House of Wisdom in Bagdhad—a gathering place for scholars who brought ancient knowledge from across the world, translated and studied it, and increased discoveries and inventions for the benefit of humanity.

◀ Sabuncuoğlu Şerafeddin (1385–1468), an Ottoman surgeon and physician, is most famous for his book Imperial Surgery, the first-ever illustrated surgical atlas

## Leading Lights

Ibn-Sina or Avicenna (980–1037) was a doctor, philosopher, scientist and author of 450 books! Most famously, he wrote *The Book of Healing* and *The Canon of Medicine*. He is considered the Father of Modern Medicine. Al-Razi or Rhazes (c. 854–935) was another great doctor and philosopher. He discovered sulphuric acid, allergic asthma, and established the use of alcohol in medicine. The amazing Al-Biruni (973–1050) excelled in physics, mathematics, astronomy, natural sciences, history, and languages. He was sought by many rulers for advice and to conduct research. Ibn-Rushd or Averroes (1126–98) was a judge and court doctor well versed in philosophy, theology, medicine, astronomy, physics, law, and languages.

▼ An illustration from Al-Biruni's writings on astronomy explains the different phases of the moon

▲ In 1017, Al-Biruni travelled to India, explored Hinduism and authored a study of Indian culture

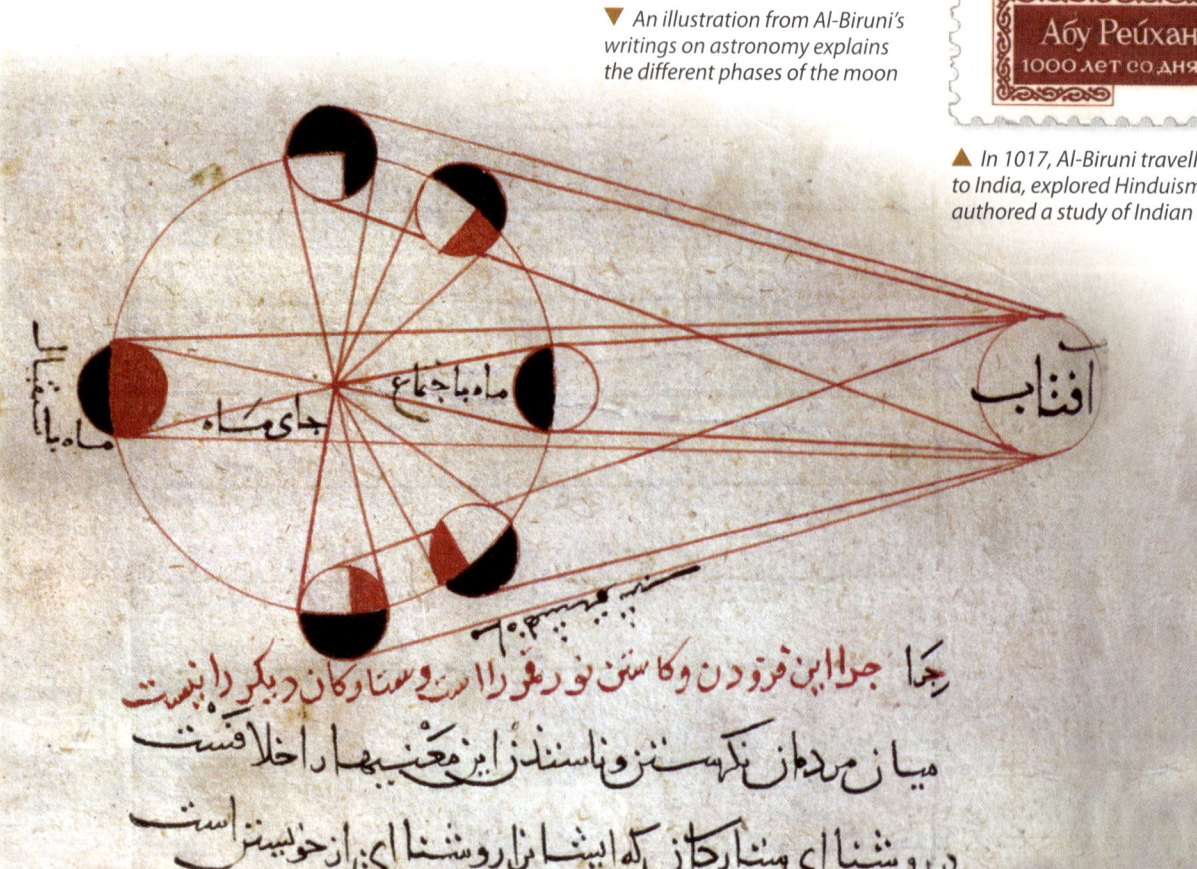

## Muslims of Ghazni

Ghazni is a city, beside the river Ghazni, on a high plateau in Afghanistan. During the 10th century, its Muslim rulers, who belonged to an aggressive Turkish dynasty, raided land around Peshawar and even threatened India. Most dreaded among them was Mahmud (971–1030), whose 33 year long reign saw some 12–17 Indian campaigns that destroyed temples and plundered Hindu treasures. After his death, his empire in Afghanistan and eastern Persia fell to a new wave of Turkish tribesmen—the Seljuks.

▶ *The painting shows an Indian raja being captured and presented before Sultan Mahmud of Ghazni*

## The Seljuk Turks

In the late 10th century, a group of Turkish tribes, led by a chieftain called Seljuk, swept down the northern borders of the Persian Empire. They converted to Islam and set about conquering an empire for themselves. In 1040, Togrul Beg, a grandson of Seljuk, took Ghazni from Mahmud's son Masud. By 1055, he had conquered the Iranian plateau and Baghdad. The new empire reached its peak around 1092 under Beg's grand-nephew Malik Shah. It stretched from Afghanistan to the Mediterranean, with some Turkish tribes finally occupying the area that would become Turkey one day.

▲ *The Great Seljuk Empire at its peak, upon the death of Malik Shah I in 1092*

## The Hashshashin

Soon after Malik Shah's death, Persia was pushed into chaos by a sinister new group called the Hashshashin, or Assassins. These are more correctly known as the Nizari Ismailis. They came into power in the 11th century by seizing fortresses in Persia. In particular, they took over the formidable stronghold of Alamut. By the 12th century, they were also secure in Syria. Rather than battling armies, the Assassins used a vast network of spies and terrorists to infiltrate and destroy enemy camps. This troublesome sect was finally quashed between two great rival powers of the 12th century—the Mamluk sultans of Egypt and the Mongol hordes of Hulagu Khan.

▶ *Rudkhan Castle in Iran was once an Assassin stronghold*

# Saxons and Normans

After the ancient Romans left, the British Isles were ruled by tribal chieftains who vied with each other for power. The Anglo-Saxons dominated England from 550–1066. They confronted **Celtic** chiefs in Wales. In the 5th century, the semi-historical **Niall of the Nine Hostages** established the kings of Ireland. In Scotland, the Picts and Scots came together under a king during the 9th century.

## Alfred and the Norsemen

In the 9th century, England faced repeated raids from sea-faring Vikings who swept down from Scandinavia. Over 865–876 CE, the Great Danish Army invaded England and defeated the kingdoms of East Anglia, Mercia, and Northumbria. Alfred of Wessex (849–99 CE), later known as Alfred the Great, rallied Saxon forces and forced the invaders back to a region called Danelaw. England finally united under Alfred's son (Edward the Elder) and grandson (Æthelstan).

▲ The Norman Conquest is recorded in the Bayeux Tapestry, commissioned by Bishop Odo of Bayeux, half-brother to William the Conqueror

▲ To establish the Kingdom of England, Alfred the Great built up the borders; established laws, education, and a navy; and reformed the English economy

## The Norman Conquest

In 1066, William, the fearsome Duke of Normandy (in France), landed on English shores, determined to take the throne. He defeated the newly crowned Harold Godwinson at the Battle of Hastings and captured the city of London. On 25th December, William was crowned as the King of England. He controlled his new kingdom by building strategically placed castles and giving power to his Norman followers. William the Conqueror is the founder of the current line of British monarchs.

### 💡 Isn't It Amazing!

The Saxons got their name from their short sword, the scramasax. Saxon lands were divided into shires, which were further divided into 'hundreds'. The peacekeeping officer of a shire was called the shire reeve. This later became our modern word sheriff.

▼ An Anglo-Saxon village

## Norman Rule

In 1085, William ordered a full survey of England. His men travelled the kingdom, recording who owned what property—land, livestock, farm equipment, mills, and so on. The findings were entered into the *Domesday Book* which William used to tax and control the people. William's heirs focussed on conquering Wales, Scotland, and Ireland. Henry II (1133–89) set up English administration in Dublin, Ireland. Wales was suppressed by Edward I (1239–1307) in the late 13th century. Scotland, however, remained independent, until its King James VI (1566–1625) inherited the English throne after the famous Queen Elizabeth!

▲ In 1215, the unpopular King John (1166–1216) was forced to sign the first charter of rights, the Magna Carta. Among many rights that it offered, the promise of swift justice and protection of barons from illegal imprisonment were the popular ones

▲ Over the late 13th and early 14th centuries, Scotland fought against English dominance in a series of military campaigns that saw heroes such as Sir William Wallace (c. 1270–1305) and King Robert the Bruce (1274–1329)

## The War of the Roses

Over 1455–87, two sides of the royal family fought for the throne leading to civil war in England. It began after the death of Henry V, the hero of Agincourt, when his successor proved to be mentally ill. The House of Lancaster was represented by a red rose and the House of York by a white rose. The wars ended when Henry Tudor defeated Richard III at the Battle of Bosworth on 22 August 1485. Henry was a grandson of Catherine (widow of Henry V) and her second husband, the Welshman, Owen Tudor. After being crowned as Henry VII, he married Elizabeth of York, thus, uniting the Lancastrian and Yorkist lines. His Tudor Dynasty marks the end of English Middle Ages. In the following years, his son and granddaughter—Henry VIII and Elizabeth I—oversaw England's Golden Age.

◀ The Battle of Bosworth, the last significant battle in the Wars of the Roses, was fought on 22 August 1485. Henry Tudor's Lancastrian forces overthrew King Richard III, who became the last English king to die in battle

▲ King Edward III initially led raids into France, burning farms and looting cities. Such medieval charges by heavily armed knights on horseback were called chevauchées

◀ The English longbow could fire faster and farther than the French crossbow. It was greatly responsible for the English victory at the Battle of Crécy (and later at Agincourt)

# The Hundred Years' War

**Over 1337–1453, French and English kings fought to control land that is now part of France.** When Charles IV of France died childless, Edward III of England demanded the French throne as his closest living relative. The French, however, refused to have a foreign king and crowned a cousin of the old king's who later became Philip IV of France. Edward responded by going to war!

##  Early English Victories

With 17 million people, and support from Scotland, France was stronger than England from the start. Yet, the English won the naval Battle of Sluys in 1340. All wars after this were fought on French soil. Under the leadership of Edward III's son—Edward, the Black Prince—England won the 1346 Battle of Crécy and the 1356 Battle of Poitiers. The prince even captured King John II of France!

##  Battle of Agincourt

The most famous battle of the period was fought in 1415 by 8,000 Englishmen (led by Henry V) against 36,000 trained French soldiers (belonging to Charles VI). Despite the odds, the English decimated the French army! When the battle began, the heavily armoured French knights found their horses slipping in mud because it had rained the previous night. The English archers rained down arrows upon them and used pointed stakes hammered into the ground to injure the charging cavalry. Some 6,000 French soldiers died and one-third of their nobility was killed or captured.

## ★ Incredible Individuals

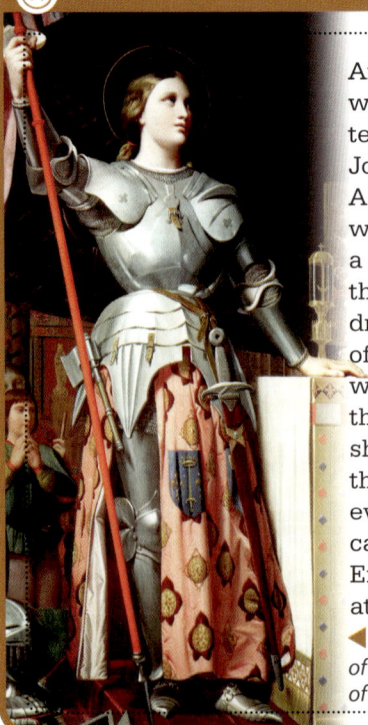

After Agincourt, France was rescued from her terrible state by St. Joan of Arc (1412–31). A young peasant girl, who was inspired by a divine vision to lead the French army and drive the English out of France. Sadly, she was abandoned by the French king after she helped him gain the crown. Joan was eventually betrayed and captured and sold to the English, who burned her at the stake.

◀ She was known as The Maid of Orléans, and died at the age of 19

# Medieval Africa

**African history of the Middle Ages has been passed on in folklore rather than being written down.** Egypt (in North Africa) is, of course, an exception. Fortunately, Muslim travellers like Ibn Batuta (c. 1304–68) left records of their journeys to Africa. Medieval Africa was a vibrant network of kingdoms where goods and ideas were exchanged. Arab scholar al-Bakri wrote admiringly of Ghana in the 11th century and Ibn Khaldun investigated the history of Mali in the 14th century.

## Islamic Africa

Merchants travelling down the Red Sea and eastern coast spread Islam to Africa. Ruins of an 8th-century wooden mosque can be seen as far south as Kenya, along with Persian pottery and Chinese stoneware. In the 11th century, a Muslim dynasty ruled along the coast of modern Tanzania. Its coins named the ruler as 'the majestic Sultan Ali Bin al-Hasan'. Ibn Batuta wrote about this prosperous sultanate with its vast trade in gold and slaves. Merchants travelling along the oasis routes of Sahara in search of gold, ivory, and salt also spread Islam to western Africa. Its first Muslim ruler was the early 11th century king of Gao. Ibn Batuta, visiting Mali in 1352, expressed mixed feelings about African practices, such as masked dancers and scantily clad women, mingling with Islamic ones.

▲ It was common practice for kingdoms to fight wars using slaves as soldiers. Amazingly, some mamluk (slave) generals used their power to set up the formidable Mamluk Dynasty that ruled Egypt and Syria from 1250 to 1517

### Incredible Individuals

It is said that the richest man on earth during the Middle Ages was Mansa Musa (c. 1280–1337), the ruler of Mali in West Africa. He was famous throughout Europe and the Middle East. He was also famous for his pilgrimage to Mecca in 1324–25. His caravan of over 60,000 people included 500 slaves—each with a gold staff—and 100 camels bearing great mounds of gold dust. Mansa Musa freely gave away so much gold that the precious metal became cheaper, and it was many years before gold increased in value again!

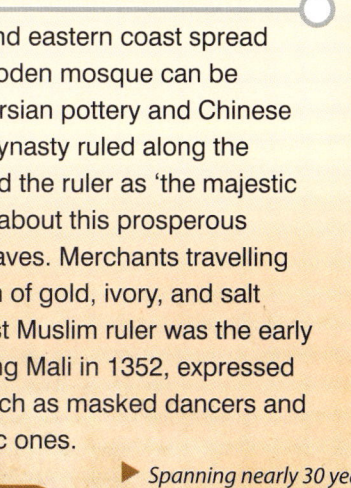

▶ Spanning nearly 30 years, the Moroccan scholar-explorer Ibn Batuta visited the Islamic nations, and even non-Islamic lands in India and China

# The Crusades

The High Middle Ages was a time when European Christians launched a series of religious wars against Muslims to capture the holy city of Jerusalem. These were called the Crusades. Historians recognise eight major Crusades between 1096 and 1291.

◀ Going to the Crusades was referred to as 'taking the cross' and Crusaders marched wearing a red cross on their clothing and banners

## The First Crusade

In 1095, Pope Urban II called on all Christians to rise against the Islamic forces of the Seljuk Turks and recapture the Holy Land. The response was tremendous! Thousands of ordinary citizens, trained knights, and noblemen joined the martial pilgrimage. Four armies were formed under the leaders Raymond of Saint-Gilles, Godfrey of Bouillon, Hugh of Vermandois, and Bohemond of Taranto. A more haphazard band of knights and commoners set off under the command of the preacher, Peter the Hermit. They were called the People's Crusade.

### 1095–1099

### 1147–1149

### Isn't It Amazing!

Over 1097–98, the Crusaders and Byzantines marched through Seljuk lands in Anatolia (Turkey) and Syria, capturing key cities like Antioch and the Seljuk capital Nicea (modern-day Iznik). To govern the vast territory, four large Crusader states were established in Jerusalem, Edessa, Antioch, and Tripoli.

▲ The capture of Jerusalem during the First Crusade was accompanied by the massacre and burning of many innocent Muslim and Jewish defenders of the city

## The Second Crusade

In 1144, the Seljuk general Zangi recaptured Edessa (in modern Turkey), stunning the other Crusader states. Pope Eugenius III announced the Second Crusade. It was led by King Louis VII of France and King Conrad III of Germany. After a series of defeats, Louis and Conrad attacked Damascus with 50,000 men. Damascus's ruler called Zangi's successor, Nur al-Din, for aid. Together, they sent the Christian army packing.

▶ Conrad III (1093–1152) was the first King of Germany from the Hohenstaufen Dynasty

## The Third Crusade

In 1169, Nur al-Din's forces—under the command of General Shirkuh and his nephew Saladin—seized Cairo, Egypt. Soon after, Saladin became Sultan and began retaking the Crusader states and Jerusalem. His troops won a decisive battle at Hattin in 1187, which sparked the Third Crusade. The Christian hero this time was King Richard I of England. In 1191, Richard the Lionheart won against Saladin in the Battle of Arsuf, recaptured the city of Jaffa and re-established some degree of Christian control. In the end, Richard was unable to conquer Jerusalem.

◀ *Saladin spares the life of Guy of Lusignan the King of Jerusalem, after Battle of Hattin*

## The Fourth Crusade

Formed by Pope Innocent III, the Fourth Crusade never even made it to the Holy Land! The Crusaders ended up looting their Christian allies in Constantinople instead. Many stayed on to set up Crusader states in Byzantine territory.

▲ *Crusaders lay siege to Constantinople in 1204*

**1187–1192**  **1202–1204**  **1208–1271**

## The Final Crusades

The later Crusades met with no success. Some were even aimed at (non-Catholic) Christians! In 1212, a group of children, women, elderly, and poor began a Children's Crusade that didn't get far. Pope Innocent III launched the Fifth Crusade in 1216 against Egypt. The land-and-sea conquest ended with the Crusaders surrendering to Saladin's nephew, Al-Malik al-Kamil, in 1221. In the Sixth Crusade (1229), Emperor Frederick II acquired Jerusalem from al-Kamil through diplomacy. When their treaty expired, the Muslims took back the city. Over 1248–54, Louis IX of France took the Seventh Crusade to Egypt, but the battle met with failure. Louis launched the Eighth Crusade in 1270 after the Mamluk Sultan Baybars demolished Antioch. The mission never reached Syria and Louis died in Tunis, Africa. In 1291, the city of Acre fell to the Mamluks. Historians mark this as the end of the Crusader states.

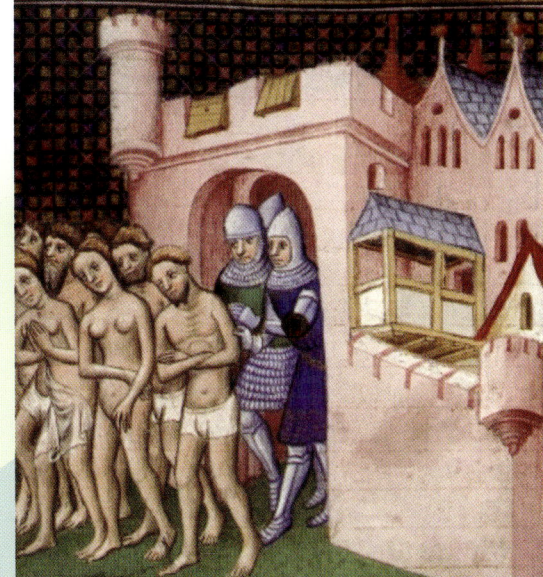

▶ *The Albigensian Crusade (1209–1229) was aimed at France's Cathari Christians seen here being expelled from Carcassonne*

# Boyars and Magyars

**In medieval Russia and many Eastern European countries like Bulgaria, boyars were members of the ruling nobility.** They held important posts in the military and formed a council to advise the Tsar (emperor of Russia). The Carpathian regions belong to the Romanians. Their boyars comprised of judges and leaders who were duly elected until the role became hereditary. The ethnic people of Hungary are called Magyars. They have occupied the Hungarian land for most of the second millennium.

▶ The funeral of a Rus chieftain on a ship, as described by the Arab traveller Ahmad ibn Fadlan in the 10th century

## Medieval Hungary (896–1526)

The Magyars established Hungary in 896 CE. Their leader Prince Arpad established the first royal house. In 1000 CE, the country became a kingdom with the crowing of its first king, Saint Stephen. Tatars (Mongols) attacked the lands in 1241 and the house of Arpad was wiped out in 1301. One of the greatest kings in the following years was Matthias Corvinus, who protected Hungary against Ottoman aggression. A decade after his death, the Ottomans split Hungary in the Battle of Mohács (1526). The western and northern areas remained under Hungary occupancy; the southern lands fell to the Ottomans; and the eastern regions became semi-independent as the Principality of Transylvania.

### Isn't It Amazing!

The land south of the Carpathians and north of River Danube became a state called Wallachia. Its most famous ruler was Vlad III (1431–76), gruesomely called Vlad the Impaler because impaling those who offended him on a stake was his favorite mode of punishment. He often arranged groups of staked bodies in favorite patterns, such as a ring outside of the city. The Romanians called him Dracul, meaning the devil.

▲ Vlad Tepes's bloodthirsty life inspired Irish author Bram Stoker to pen his Gothic masterpiece, Dracula

## Kievan Rus

The powerful empire called Kievan Rus centred around the city of Kiev during the Middle Ages. In coming times which would eventually form Russia and Ukraine. Its people were originally Vikings who migrated to Eastern Europe in the 9th century. They established a kingdom under King Rurik whose dynasty ruled Rus for 900 years! In 880, King Oleg made Kiev his capital and set out in expanding the empire. He even raided Byzantium and Constantinople, but finally made peace with them.

◀ *A monument to princes Rurik and Oleg in Old Ladoga, Russia*

## Golden Age of Kievan Rus

The rule of Vladimir the Great (c. 958–1015) and Yaroslav the Wise (c. 978–1054) marked the Golden Age of the empire. Vladimir united many of the Slavic states under his rule and converted to Christianity. This strengthened his ties with Constantinople, which, in turn, increased the flow of trade and knowledge. Kievan Rus reached its peak under the rule of mighty Yaroslav the Wise, whose wise administration policies induced the strength of military and gave boost to the cultural development. Yaroslav codified the laws, built a library, and promoted education. After his death, the Mongols invaded the land, bringing an end to the unity of Rus.

### In Real Life

The boyars were at the height of their power in the Middle Ages. Tsar Ivan the Terrible brought them to heel in the 16th century. Tsar Peter the Great further curbed their powers by abolishing the council of advisors in 1711.

▶ *Tsar Ivan the Terrible (1530–1584)*

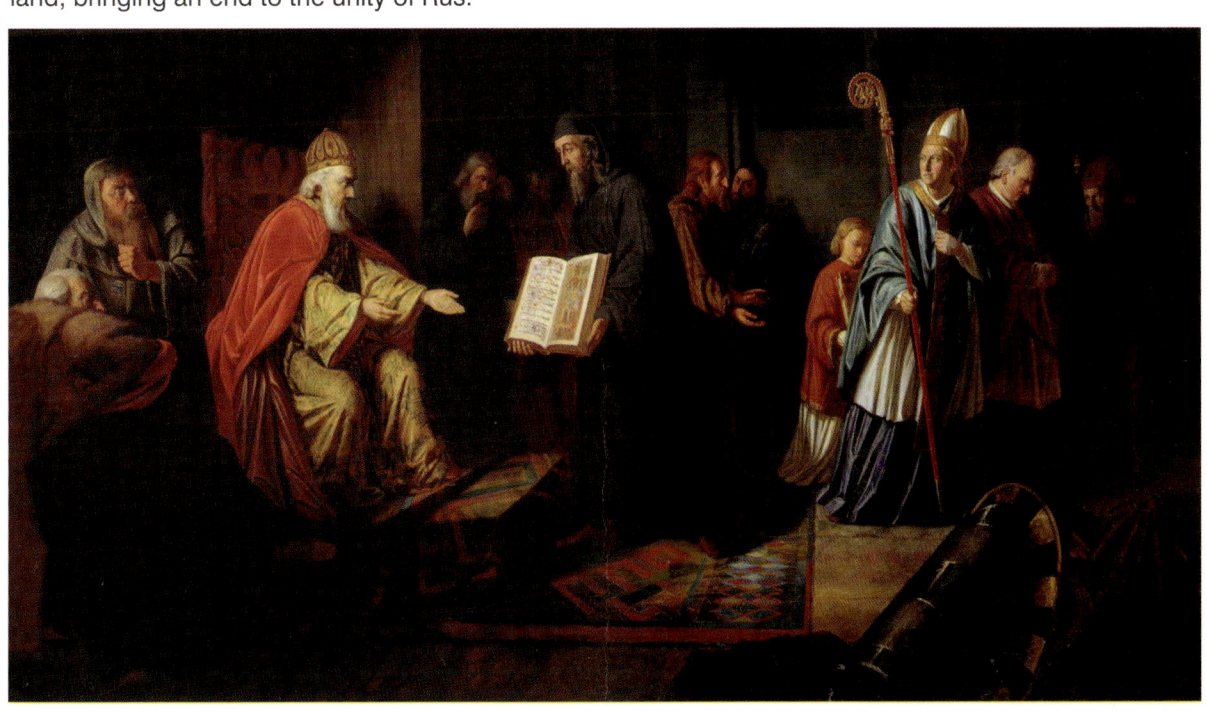

◀ *Vladimir considered many religions before choosing Christianity! Ivan Eggink's painting shows him listening to the Orthodox priests, while the papal envoy stands aside in discontent*

# Mongol Hordes

**The Mongolian steppes were home to nomadic empires such as the Xiongnu (3rd century BCE–1st century CE), Xianbei (c. 93–234 CE), Rouran Khaganate (330–555), Turkic Khaganate (552–744) and others.** In Central Asia, the Khitan group established the Liao Dynasty (907–1125), which ruled Mongolia and parts of Russia, Korea, and China. The various tribes finally united in 1206 under a man named Temujin (1162–1227), who was renamed Genghis Khan and was elected on the banks of the Onon River. Genghis Khan's army of warriors is remembered today as the Mongol horde!

▲ *A 14th century portrait of Genghis Khan, the fearsome founder of the Mongol Empire*

## The Khan's Empire

Genghis Khan became the ruler of a huge sweep of land which extended from Asia to the Adriatic sea. His descendants expanded the empire, conquering places as far-flung as Poland and Vietnam. At its height, the Mongol Empire was about the size of Africa! Though Genghis Khan is chiefly remembered for the terror of his invasions, he was also a good ruler to his subjects. He allowed religious freedom, abolished torture, encouraged trade, and set up the first international postal system. He died in 1227 during a campaign against the Chinese kingdom of Xi Xia.

## The Khatuns

Genghis Khan's vast empire was ruled by women—by the Khan's aunts, daughters, and consorts! Throughout his life, he had been protected and enabled by women. He trusted them to rule well and not betray him. Defeated kings were forced to join the horde to conquer other parts of the world. Meanwhile, the Khan women were brought in to administer the land, sign treaties, suppress rebellions, and pass judgements. Genghis Khan's daughters ended up controlling the valuable Silk Route. They gave him aid for his campaigns in China and Persia. His daughter Altani was even made 'Hero Ba'atur', a title given to military and political champions. Sadly, after the Khan's death, his heirs neglected his legacy.

◀ *Gold dinari from Genghis Khan's time struck at Ghazni in 1221–1222*

◀ *Members of various tribes bow to Genghis Khan as he is elected ruler of the Mongols*

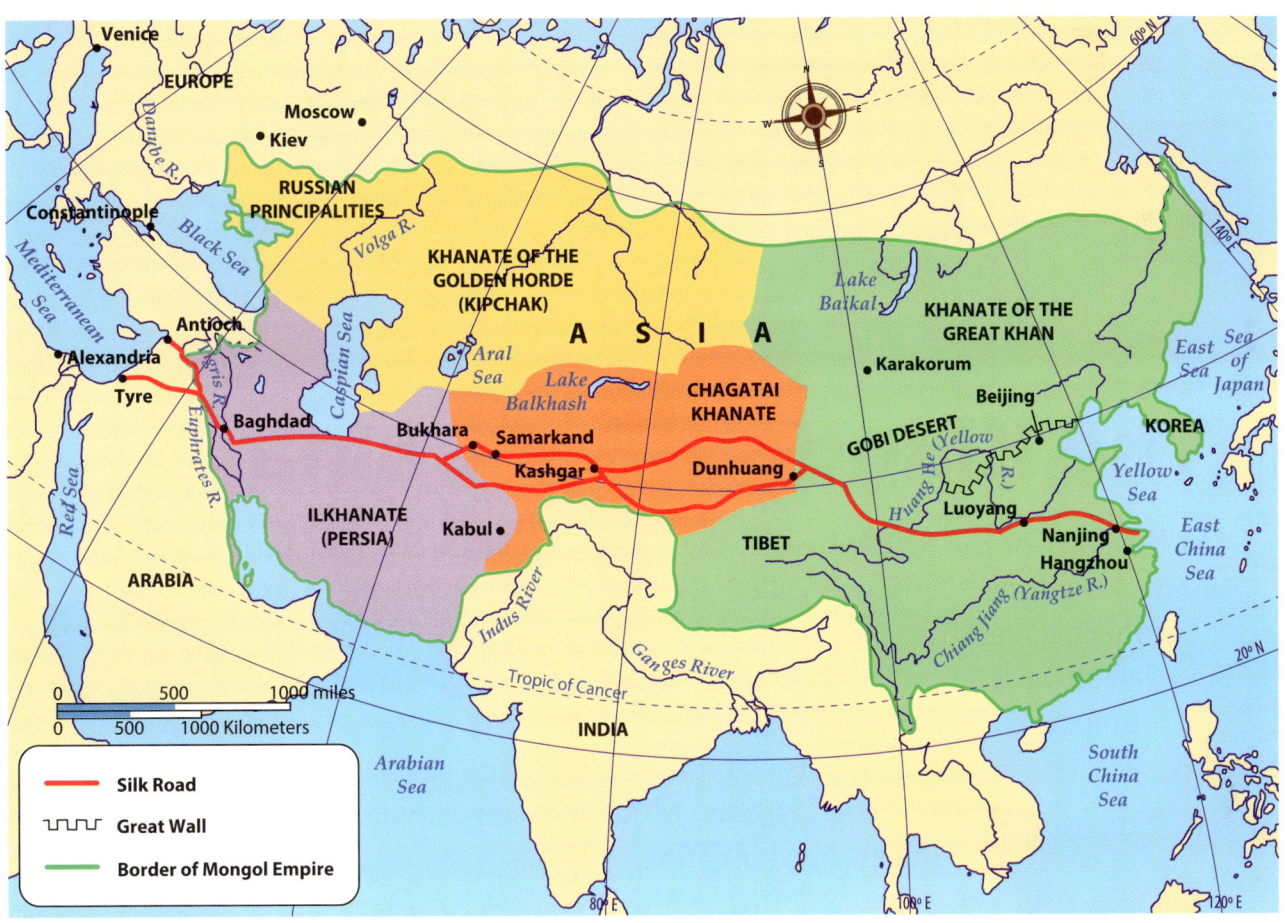

▲ *The Silk Road in the Mongol Khanates in 1294 CE*

##  The Mongol Khanates

The great conqueror's grandchildren settled in three increasingly independent regions. Kublai Khan, as the Great Khan, had the grandest realm. His brother Hulagu ruled the Ilkanate lands of Persia and Mesopotamia. His cousins, the brothers Batu and Berke, moved with the Golden Horde to Polish and Russian territories. The horde's name here seems to have come from the golden tent used by Batu. In Central Asia, Genghis's second son ruled a fourth realm called Chagatai Khaganate.

## The Yuan Dynasty of China

From 1252 onwards, Kublai Khan pressed southwards through mountains to China. In 1264, he became the Great Khan, which gave him more resources to conquer China. In 1271, he moved the imperial capital to Beijing and built a magnificent city. Mongols called it Khanbaliq—the city of the Khan. From this base, he overwhelmed the Song Dynasty and became the first Mongol-Chinese emperor of the new Yuan Dynasty. His reign and empire became famous through the writings of the Italian merchant Marco Polo, who spent many years in the Mongol court.

### In Real Life

Over the 14th century, Mongol power all but disappeared. The last Il-Khan died in 1335. The Yuan Dynasty fell to the Ming Dynasty in 1368. In 1380, the grand prince of Moscow defeated the Golden Horde in a battle on Kulikovo Plain. The Mongols hung on for another two centuries, but they were now competing with many rising rivals.

▼ *Kublai Khan, wearing Mongol-style furs over Han Chinese silk brocades, out on a hunting expedition*

# The Kingdoms of China

**At the start of the Middle Ages, the Chinese lands were split into many kingdoms.** This was called the period of the Northern and Southern Dynasties. The man who reunited China in 589 CE established the Sui Dynasty. He took the title Wen Di (Cultured Emperor). The dynasty was overthrown in 618 CE by one of the emperor's high officials. He established the Tang Dynasty, which oversaw a dynamic Golden Age for China.

▲ *Eighty-seven Celestials, the draft painting of a fresco by master artist Wu Daozi (c. 685–758)*

◀ *Yang Di, the second Sui emperor, famously constructed the Grand Canal—the longest and oldest artificial river in the world*

## Incredible Individuals

Wu Zetian (c. 625–705) was the only woman to rule China in her own right. A concubine of the powerful Emperor Taizong, she later became empress to his more feeble heir, Emperor Gaozong. After his death, she became the sole ruler of the Zhou Dynasty, which began and ended with her. Empress Wu had a large and loyal network of spies who enabled her to rule successfully. A ruthless empress, she employed talented people and made smart decisions.

▲ *The Fengxian cave of the Longmen Grottoes, commissioned by Wu Zetian, who made Buddhism the state religion*

## Tang Dynasty (618–907)

Chinese culture under the Tang Dynasty reached new heights, particularly in ceramics and literature. The Japanese adopted the Chinese way of writing at this time, modifying the characters to suit their own language. Imperial China controlled all land from the northwest desert oases of the Silk Road to parts of Manchuria in the northeast and Vietnam in the south. Princes as far off as Bukhara and Samarkand recognised the emperor's sovereignty. The dynasty weakened after the devastating **An Lushan Rebellion** (755–763). Later many more rebellions followed. Most shockingly, in 878–79, a rebel army trying to overthrow the Tang massacred tens of thousands of people in the port city of Guangzhou.

▶ *The Tang period is famous for its sancai (three-colour) ceramics, as seen in this fierce tomb guardian*

##  Song Dynasty (960–1279)

After the Tang, China split into many states. This was the Five Dynasties and Ten Kingdoms Period (907–960). It ended when a warlord took over and established the Song Dynasty. Paper money, which had come into use shortly before, became a familiar currency during the Song rule. The emperors encouraged civilian administrators and reduced the power of military lords. Over time, Song rule made the nation most sophisticated. However, it also weakened China. The Songs were finally overthrown by Kublai Khan and his Mongol Yuan Dynasty.

▶ The design of the Chinese sailing ships (called junks) was perfected during the later Song period. Its pioneering features such as the bulkhead, the sternpost rudder, watertight hulls and multiple masts were copied around the world

##  The Ming Dynasty (1368–1644)

Kublai Khan's grandson and successor managed to keep order in the Yuan Empire. But a number of disasters in the early 14th century made it weaker. There were serious issues that sprouted such as a war between rival Mongol princes, widespread famine, and disastrous floods, that ultimately resulted into a massive rebellion. In 1368, Zhu Yuanzhang, a Buddhist monk and rebel leader, captured Beijing and sent the Mongols flying back to their native grasslands. He called his new empire, Ming (brilliant). Chinese explorations under Ming reached as far west as Africa and the Middle East. They are to be credited for building the famous Forbidden City of Beijing. China became famous for its exquisite porcelain, lacquer, silks, gold, silver, and medicines.

◀ A troop of pike-wielding Ming soldiers ferry across a river

# Medieval India

**The collapse of the Gupta Empire (480–550 CE) marks the start of the medieval period in India.** This was marked by wars among the regional kingdoms and a series of invasions by the Afghans and Turks.

## The Fight for Kannauj

The Pratihara Dynasty ruled most of India over the 6th–11th centuries. Their capital was at Kannauj. The empire reached its peak under Mihira Bhoja (836–85) and Mahendrapala I (885–910). The empire's expansion triggered a three-way power struggle with the Rashtrakuta Empire (from the south) and Pala Empire (from the east) for control of the Indian subcontinent and of Kannauj over the 8th–10th centuries.

▲ The tripartite fight for Kannauj and the Gangetic Plains in the early medieval period

## Chola Champions

One of the longest-ruling dynasties in history, the Cholas became a military, economic and cultural power under Rajaraja Chola I, his son Rajendra Chola I, and their immediate successors. Their mighty kingdom traversed from up east to the Ganges and across the oceans to Southeast Asia. The Chola fleet represented the height of medieval Indian sea power.

◄ Sala (founder of the empire) fighting the tiger is the emblem of the Hoysala Empire (10th–14th centuries). They were known for exquisite architecture as seen here in Chennakeshava Temple, Belur

▶ Early medieval India saw the rise of Rajput clans like the Gurjara-Pratihara, who are most famous for temples such as the one at Khajuraho, now a UNESCO World Heritage Site

##  The Delhi Sultanate

For 320 years, the Delhi Sultanate stretched over large parts of India. The period saw five dynasties—the Mamluk (1206–90), Khilji (1290–1320), Tughlaq (1320–1414), Sayyid (1414–51), and Lodi (1451–1526). Qutb ud-Din Aibak, a former *mamluk* (slave) of Muhammad Ghori, became the first sultan of Delhi. His Mamluk Dynasty is not to be confused with the other powerful Mamluk Dynasty of Egypt.

### Incredible Individuals

The Delhi sultanate enthroned one of the few female Islamic rulers, Razia Sultana (ruled 1236–40). She was five when Aibak died and her father Iltutmish took the throne. Finding that none of his sons measured up to his daughter, Iltutmish became the first sultan to appoint a woman as his heir. The Persian historian Minhaj-i-Siraj recorded that Razia Sultana was a just monarch cherished by her subjects. Sadly, she was overthrown and killed by her brother Bahram.

◀ *Coin from Razia Sultana's time*

▲ *Aibak famously commissioned the exquisite tower, the Qutb Minar, which was completed by the Khiljis*

##  The Vijayanagara Empire

Based in the Deccan Plateau, the Vijayanagara Empire was established by brothers Harihara and Bukka Raya in 1336. The empire warded off Islamic invasions, brought new technologies in water management, established a dynamic sea trade and evolved Carnatic music to its current form. It is famous today in the folktales of King Krishnadevaraya and his witty court poet Tenali Rama.

▲ *The ruins at Hampi, Vijayanagara's capital city*

# Samurai and Shogun

**Japan's first emperor, Jimmu Tenno, came to power way back in 660 BCE.** Medieval Japan is marked by the shifting of power from the emperors to military warlords called Shoguns. It also saw the rise of a warrior class called Samurai and clans of spies called Ninjas.

▲ *A silver Wadokaichin coin*

##  Asuka Period (c. 538–710 CE)

Power was centred in the Asuka region. At this time, the Chinese writing system was adopted in Japan. Buddhism was introduced from China via the Korean peninsula. In 708, a mint was set up in the province of Omi. It made coins that became the first Japanese currency.

◀ *Prince Shotoku (574–622), a semi-legendary regent of the Asuka period who is venerated even today for his virtuous and non-violent administration*

##  Nara Period (710–794 CE)

Empress Gemmei (660–721) set up a new capital in Nara, modelled on the Tang capital in China. This was a period of slow development. The emperor's family fought for power with Buddhists and other groups. Towards the end of the 8th century, Dokyo, a powerful priest-minister rose to the forefront. Fearing the dominance of priests, a family of nobles called Fujiwara rebelled. They crowned a new emperor, Konin. His successor, Emperor Kammu shifted the capital again—first to Nagaoka, and in 794 to Heian (present-day Kyoto). This helped sever connections with the temples of Nara and re-established government under the emperor's will.

▲ *The famous Daibutsu (giant Buddha) at Todai-ji, one of the Seven Great Temples of the Nara period*

##  Heian Japan (794–1185)

Imperial Japan reached its peak during the Heian period. Court life was noted for its art, poetry, and literature. The first known novel—*Genji Monogatari (The Tale of Genji)* was published in 1010. Its author was the court lady Murasaki Shikibu.

During the Heian era, the emperor disbanded his army. Gradually, his power declined. Royal descendants, such as the Fujiwara, Taira, and Minamoto families, took the chance to set up rival regimes. They hired guards, police and soldiers for their provinces. Other nobles began to follow their example. Soon, Japan had private armies that did not report to the emperor. The ensuing rebellion established the samurai warrior classes as a force to reckon with.

◀ *A 17th century sculpture of Murasaki Shikibu at her desk. She was a Japanese novelist, poet, and lady at the Imperial court during the Heian period*

# Rise of the Shogun

Over the 12th century, a series of battles took place between the noble families of Japan. This destroyed the Fujiwaras and culminated in the Genpei Wars (1180–85) between the Taira and Minamoto clans. When the Taira clan fell, Minamoto Yoritomo became the first Shogun (military ruler) of Japan.

 ## The Kamakura Period (1185-1333)

Minamoto's headquarters in Kamakura gave the first Shogunate its name. Civil, military, and judicial matters were in the hands of the Shogun and a system of feudalism—much like the one in Western Europe—was established. Two new Buddhist sects—Jodo and Zen—arose at this time.

▲ *Minamoto Yoritomo, the first Shogun*

### Isn't It Amazing!

Over 1274–81, the Japanese faced a few invasions by Mongols. In the end, the Japanese were saved by the weather. Kublai Khan's 600 ships and 23,000 troops were destroyed by typhoons! Shinto priests called this phenomenon *kamikaze*—divine wind!

◀ *The samurai Suenaga facing Mongol and Korean arrows and bombs*

## The Muromachi Period (1336-1573)

The emperor's power was briefly brought back during the Kenmu Restoration. However, his allies, who brought down the Kamakura Shogunate in 1333, were ambitious warlords. The Ashikaga Takauji (1305-58) finally drove the emperor from his court and supported a new emperor who, in turn, installed Ashikaga as the new Shogun. The third Ashikaga Shogun shifted his residence to Muromachi, which gives its name to this historical period.

▲ *A wooden Kongorikishi, a muscular guardian of the Buddha, from the 14th century Kamakura Shogunate*

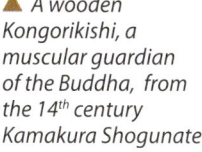

▶ *China's Ming Dynasty sought help from the Muromachi Shogun to suppress Japanese pirates along coastal China*

*Ashikaga Takauji*

# Word Check

**Abbess:** This was the senior, the leader, of all nuns in a convent.

**Abbot:** This was the senior, the leader, of all monks in a monastery.

**An Lushan Rebellion:** General An Lushan went against the Tang emperor and made himself the emperor of northern China in 755 CE. His Yan Dynasty fell in 763 CE, but the fight greatly weakened his Tang rivals.

**Caliph:** It refers to the Islamic rulers who succeeded the Prophet Muhammad. The word comes from Arabic kalifa, meaning deputy of God.

**Celtic:** A collection of cultures/peoples, including Picts and Scots, who settled in the British Isles and parts of Spain. They are known today by their culture and languages (e.g. Irish, Scottish Gaelic, and Welsh).

**Cloisonné:** A decorative work in which enamel, glass, or gemstones are separated by strips of flattened wire on a metal backing.

**Gaul:** The ancient name for France.

**Guilds:** Professional groups formed by people of a trade.

**Hundred Years' War:** This was a series of European conflicts, divided by short periods of truce. It was spread over a century; hence the name.

**Iberian Peninsula:** The south-westernmost peninsula of Europe, comprising Spain and Portugal.

**Nativity:** The occasion of a person's birth, most often used to refer to the birth of Jesus Christ.

**Niall of the Nine Hostages:** A part-historical, part-legendary king of the northern half of Ireland. He lived sometime during the $4^{th}$–$5^{th}$ centuries CE.

**Nika riots:** Many people, unhappy with Emperor Justinian I's reforms, tried to overthrow him. They shouted 'Nika!' (Conquer!) and assaulted the palace. Half the city burned and thousands died before the riots were quelled.

**Patriarchal:** Relating to a system or government that is controlled by men.

**Polymath:** A person of wide and varied learning.

**Purgatory:** In Catholicism, this means a temporary place of suffering for dead souls of sinners before they go to heaven.

**Sacking:** This is the capturing and plundering of cities by invading armies.

**Schism:** This is a word for discord that leads to a formal division/splitting of a group.

**Serf:** In feudal times, workers were often compelled to serve their landowners without pay, as if they were their property, much like slaves. Such bonded labourers were called serfs.

**Siege:** This is when an army blockades an enemy's city or fort, cutting off communication and supplies to force it to surrender.